Warrior Women in American History

THE ROLE OF FEMALE PILOTS IN WORLD WAR II

Cavendish Square

New York

Hallie Murray

Published in 2020 by Cavendish Square Publishing, LLC

243 5th Avenue, Suite 136, New York, NY 10016

Copyright © 2020 by Cavendish Square Publishing, LLC

First Edition

No part of this publication may be reproduced, stored in a retrieval system, or transmitted in any form or by any means—electronic, mechanical, photocopying, recording, or otherwise—without the prior permission of the copyright owner. Request for permission should be addressed to Permissions, Cavendish Square Publishing, 243 5th Avenue, Suite 136, New York, NY 10016. Tel (877) 980-4450; fax (877) 980-4454.

Website: cavendishsq.com

This publication represents the opinions and views of the author based on his or her personal experience, knowledge, and research. The information in this book serves as a general guide only. The author and publisher have used their best efforts in preparing this book and disclaim liability rising directly or indirectly from the use and application of this book.

All websites were available and accurate when this book was sent to press.

Cataloging-in-Publication Data
Names: Murray, Hallie.
Title: The role of female pilots in World War II / Hallie Murray.
Description: New York : Cavendish Square Publishing, 2020. | Series: Warrior women in American history | Includes glossary and index.
Identifiers: ISBN 9781502655462 (pbk.) | ISBN 9781502655479 (library bound) | ISBN 9781502655486 (ebook)
Subjects: LCSH: Women Airforce Service Pilots (U.S.)–Biography–Juvenile literature. | Women air pilots–United States–Biography–Juvenile literature. |
Air pilots, Military–United States–Biography–Juvenile literature. |
World War, 1939-1945–Aerial operations, American–Juvenile literature.
Classification: LCC D790.5 M87 2020 | DDC 940.54'497309252 B–dc23

Printed in China

Portions of this book originally appeared in *American Women Pilots of World War II* by Karen Donnelly.

Photo Credits: Cover, p. 3 U.S. National Archives Catalog, 342-AF-29183AC. Downloaded from Wikimedia Commons, https://en.wikipedia.org/wiki/File:Elizabeth_L._Remba_Gardner,_Women%27s_Airforce_Service_Pilots,_NARA-542191.jpg/PD; pp. 7, 86 Corbis Historical/Getty Images; pp. 10-11, 54-55 U.S. Air Force via The Abilene Reporter-News/AP Images; p. 12 Andy Cross/The Denver Post/Getty Images; p. 15 U.S. Air Force/Wikimedia Commons/File:Love 1 350.jpg/PD; pp. 18, 22-23, 49, 68-69 © AP Images; pp. 26-27 Keystone-France/Gamma-Keystone/Getty Images; pp. 28-29 U.S. National Archive Catalog, 208-N-4223. Downloaded from Wikimedia Commons, https://commons.wikimedia.org/wiki/File:Nancy_Harkness_Love_at_28.jpg/PD; p. 33 August Scherl/Hulton Archive/Getty Images; p. 35 ullstein bild/Getty Images; p. 38 Thomas D. McAvoy/The LIFE Picture Collection/Getty Images; p. 41 Central Press/Hulton Archive/Getty Images; pp. 43, 71 PhotoQuest/Archive Photos/Getty Images; p. 46 J. R. Eyerman/The LIFE Picture Collection/Getty Images; pp. 51, 88-89 Bettmann/Getty Images; pp. 58-59 Print Collector/Hulton Archive/Getty Images; p. 61 PJF Military Collection/Alamy Stock Photo; pp. 64-65 John Hoffman/Shutterstock.com; pp. 72-73, p. 81 Leonard McCombe/Picture Post/Getty Images; pp. 82-83 Imperial War Museums/Getty Images.

Warrior Women in
American History

THE ROLE OF
FEMALE
PILOTS
IN
WORLD
WAR II

Contents

Introduction

For the first two years of World War II, America remained neutral and, at least officially, uninvolved in the war in Europe. Though the United States supported the British military and the Allies in material ways, it didn't engage directly in the fighting. That all changed, though, on December 7, 1941, when Japanese planes dropped bombs on the US military base at Pearl Harbor in Hawaii. More than 2,300 American soldiers, sailors, and civilians were killed in the attack. America could no longer stand on the sidelines. By December 11, President Franklin D. Roosevelt had declared war on Japan, Germany, and Italy.

Americans were caught up in a wave of patriotism, and everyone looked for ways they could help the war effort. Young men joined the army, and women were encouraged to join the workforce to replace those young men at factory jobs and help manufacture munitions. During World War II, thousands of women entered the workforce, taking the place of all of the men who had been sent to fight for the United States in Europe. Rosie the Riveter is the iconic symbol of working women during World War II. She represents all of the women who took traditionally "male" jobs in factories and shipyards, helping to build weapons and other munitions. Between 1940 and 1944, the number of women employed in war-related industries

One of the most iconic images of World War II is Rosie the Riveter, shown here. She represents the women who replaced male workers in factories and other traditionally male workplaces.

rose 460 percent, and female membership in labor unions quadrupled. In 1942, at the Kaiser Shipyard in Portland, Oregon, women made up 60 percent of the workforce.

Two women pilots, Nancy Harkness Love and Jacqueline Cochran, proposed that women aviators might be uniquely positioned to help the war effort. They couldn't join the military, but they could help fill any available civilian positions currently held by men so that all male pilots could be called to the front to fly in combat. At the beginning of the war, the US Army Air Force had enough male pilots and turned down the proposals. However, as the war progressed and male pilots were lost, the Army Air Force reconsidered its decision. Eventually, both proposals were accepted. Two separate groups of women pilots were formed as civil service employees. In 1943, they were merged into one group—the Women Airforce Service Pilots (WASP).

When the WASP was announced, over 25,000 women with flying experience responded. Of those, 1,102 would graduate from the training program to operational duty. These women helped ferry planes from factories to air bases and carried other necessary provisions to help supply the men at the front. Unfortunately, the program was disbanded in December 1944. But the women of WASP didn't want to go home. They loved flying for their country, and they felt it was unfair that the male pilots suddenly got to take over their ferrying jobs just by virtue of gender.

It was the same in the wider world of the workplace as well: when the war ended, people worried that the women who had taken up those factory jobs so enthusiastically wouldn't want to give them up. They were right to worry—like the women of the WASP, the women working outside the home in traditionally "male" jobs were loath to give those jobs up. As soldiers began returning home, the image of working women as comrades-in-arms was replaced by the danger of women competing with men.

When it came to the WASP, the military establishment was well aware that training male pilots to replace the more experienced WASP members would take $1 million and four months. In the meantime, airplanes, especially pursuit planes, would sit on runways. Besides, the WASPs wanted to stay. Some of them had just finished training. Unfortunately, they could only continue to serve their country if they signed on for nonflying duty. About 155 WASP members made that choice. Even when ferrying commanders asked if their WASP members could stay, the army sent them home. It was unfair and sexist, but at the end of the day, the men of the War Department decided to waste time and money training inexperienced men instead of allowing women to stay in their positions as pilots helping the military.

The WASP members had been a well-kept secret. For decades, history ignored their contribution to the Allies' success. Then, in 1976, the US Air Force declared that women would begin pilot training. These would be the first women to fly United States military aircraft. The WASP were surely happy for these women, but they felt slighted. They had been the first women to fly planes for the military, but their years of service were once again being ignored.

The WASP organized a publicity campaign, and this time, they were heard. Senator Barry Goldwater sponsored a new bill in Congress that would finally give the WASP military status. Encouraged, WASP members around the country asked people to sign petitions supporting the bill.

Four members of the Women Airforce Service Pilots (WASP) (*from left to right*: Frances Green, Peg Kirchner, Ann Waldner, and Blanche Osborn) walk away from their plane after a training flight in Ohio.

This Congressional Gold Medal was awarded to WASP members throughout the country in July 2009. Three pilots walk under a plane on the left, while on the right is a bust of a WASP in flight gear.

They spoke to news reporters and government officials. On November 23, 1977, the WASP bill passed and was signed into law by President Jimmy Carter.

In 1987, Brigadier General Wilma Vaught began raising money for a memorial to recognize the military service of women. On October 18, 1997, the Women in Military Service for America Memorial was dedicated. The memorial, located at the entrance to Arlington National Cemetery in Washington, DC, is America's first major national memorial honoring women who have served in all branches of the armed forces throughout the nation's history.

In 2005, former WASP Deanie Bishop Parrish and her daughter established a museum dedicated to the WASP in Sweetwater, Texas. Then, in 2009, the WASP were honored on a national level: WASP members were inducted into the International Air & Space Hall of Fame at the San Diego Air & Space Museum. In July of that year, the WASPs were collectively awarded the Congressional Gold Medal in honor of the work they'd done for their country. It took a long time, but finally, it seemed, women pilots who had sacrificed for their country during World War II were being awarded the recognition they deserved.

Nancy Love, Leader of the WAFS

Nancy Harkness Love knew she wanted to be a pilot from a very early age. She was just sixteen when she got her pilot's license, and she continued to fly planes through the end of high school and into college. After leaving college early, she continued flying as a test pilot and racer. When World War II began, Love wanted to contribute her skills to the war effort. Women could not fly on the front lines, but Love convinced air force officials that female pilots could help ferry planes from factories to where they were needed at air bases. The resulting group of women pilots was known as the Women's Auxiliary Ferrying Squadron (WAFS), with Love at the head. Later on, the WAFS was folded into the Women Airforce Service Pilots (WASP), where Love also served as a leader. Love was instrumental in creating space for women in the air force, and she received many honors for her work during the war.

Flying Lessons

On a hot summer day in 1935, sixteen-year-old Nancy Harkness was enjoying a horseback ride in a field

Nancy Harkness Love is shown here circa 1943. Harkness started flying as a high school student and went on to become director of the WAFS.

outside her hometown of Houghton, Michigan. She heard an unusual sound and looked to the sky. A shiny, sleek airplane circled overhead, then landed nearby. The pilot was a barnstormer who made his living giving rides in his plane. Harkness paid five dollars for a short flight. That night at dinner, she told her father that she had decided to quit high school and become a pilot.

Harkness's father suggested that she take flying lessons while she was in school instead of dropping out. Nancy agreed and spent the last weeks of August logging as many hours in the air as possible. On August 31, she soloed (flew alone) for the first time. In September, she returned to her boarding school, Milton Academy, near Boston, Massachusetts.

She continued to fly while at Milton Academy and, afterward, at Vassar College in Poughkeepsie, New York. In New York, she spent weekends at the airport. She earned extra money by taking students for rides in an airplane that she rented. By the time she was twenty years old, she had earned her commercial license and her transport pilot's license. Unfortunately, Harkness's time at Vassar was cut short. Financial trouble caused by the Great Depression forced her to leave school. She got a job as the Boston-area sales representative for Beechcraft, a manufacturer of small planes based in Wichita, Kansas.

Selling airplanes, though, was not nearly as exciting as flying them. So Harkness was thrilled when, in 1935, Phoebe Omlie, special assistant for intelligence of the National Advisory Committee for Aeronautics, chose her to work with President Franklin D. Roosevelt's Works Progress Administration's Airmarking Project.

Phoebe Omlie

A pioneer in aviation, Phoebe Omlie began her aviation career as a stunt performer in and on aircraft. In fact, she set a world record for the highest-altitude parachute jump performed by a woman. She married an aviator, Vernon Omlie, in 1922, and in 1927, Omlie became the first woman to receive an airplane mechanic's license, as well as the first woman to become a licensed transport pilot in the United States. After Franklin D. Roosevelt was elected president in 1932, he appointed Omlie as the "Special Adviser for Air Intelligence to the National Advisory Committee for Aeronautics," though she resigned from that role when her husband died in a plane crash. When World War II began, Omlie returned to Washington, DC, to help Roosevelt create training schools for military pilots, and while there she was able to establish a program for training women as flight instructors. Omlie passed away in 1975 at the age of seventy-two.

In the 1930s, pilots navigated by landmarks on the ground that they could recognize from the sky. Through the Airmarking Project, the roofs of prominent buildings were painted with markers and the name of the town in which they stood. Harkness traveled the eastern part of the United States convincing town leaders to participate in the project. Later, women pilots ferrying planes across the country would use these markers to find their way.

Inter City Airways

In 1935, Harkness left her job to care for her ailing mother and to plan her wedding to Robert Love, an Army Air Corps

Phoebe Omlie stands near her Monocoupe plane after arriving in San Diego, California, on July 14, 1928, during the National Air Tour. Omlie was the only woman to participate in the tour.

Reserve officer. Love had been a student at Princeton and the Massachusetts Institute of Technology but left school to start his own company, Inter City Airways, at East Boston Airport. Inter City Airways did all kinds of things, from training new pilots to operating charter flights to selling airplanes. But Inter City had also undertaken an important role in the developing war in Europe: the company ferried airplanes from the United States to Canada. These planes would eventually be sent to England to help defend against the Germans.

Nancy Harkness Love flew for Inter City often, including to help advertise new planes to customers. Her flight on a ferrying mission for Inter City gave her an idea. She knew of at least forty-nine women pilots qualified for the same job. On May 21, 1940, she wrote to Colonel Robert Olds of the Army Air Corps Plans Division, suggesting that women pilots be used to ferry aircraft for the military. Olds was interested in the proposal, but at the time, the United States still wasn't directly involved in the war. Instead of refusing the proposal outright, Olds decided to keep it on file, just in case the idea could be useful at a later date.

Attempting to Enter the AAF

On December 7, 1941, Japanese forces attacked Pearl Harbor, bringing the United States into the war. Suddenly, the need for trained pilots increased dramatically. After Pearl Harbor, all airports along the East Coast were shut down, including Boston-area airports, grounding Inter City Airways. Bob Love was placed on active duty with the Air Transport Command (ATC), headquartered in Washington, DC. In 1942, he and Nancy moved to Washington, where she found a job working in the Baltimore, Maryland, office of the ATC's Ferrying Command.

Surprisingly, war rationing made it easier for Nancy to get gasoline for an airplane than for a car. So she commuted the 60 miles (96 kilometers) from Washington to Baltimore each day by plane. At the same time, Colonel William Tunner, commander of the ATC, was on a desperate hunt for pilots. When he heard from Bob Love that his wife was a pilot, the idea of using women on ferrying missions was reborn. A few days later, Colonel Tunner met with Nancy. She drafted a new proposal that he submitted to Brigadier General Harold George.

Her proposal included hiring women on the same basis as men—with the same qualifications, at the same salary, and with the same training program. The ATC, however, didn't like this plan and wanted to impose more restrictions on women, requiring more flying time and a high school diploma. Nancy Harkness Love reluctantly agreed. Because of these extra conditions, her recruits were more qualified than many men at the same level, but they were still only allowed to fly the smallest airplanes. To add insult to injury, the women would be restricted to one ferry base in New Castle, Delaware, rather than combined with squadrons of male pilots.

The obstacles didn't end there. Love, General George, and Colonel Tunner assumed that women, like men, would be hired as civilians, trained for ninety days, and then commissioned into the Army Air Force (AAF). By June, however, the AAF had a women's auxiliary, the Women's Auxiliary Army Corps (WAAC). Love proposed that pilots could be part of this organization instead of the AAF. Unfortunately, the laws establishing the WAAC did not provide flight pay or flying officers, meaning women pilots could not be officially commissioned until Congress passed a new law, a process that could take months.

Colonel Tunner needed pilots badly, so he asked Love to move ahead even though the future of the program was uncertain. She agreed, promising an initial squadron of twenty-five pilots which would be known as the Women's Auxiliary Ferrying Squadron (WAFS). These women would be hired as civil service employees, but Tunner and Love both hoped that Congress would act as soon as possible to amend the WAAC legislation so that female pilots could be paid and commissioned just as the men of the AAF program were.

The Women's Auxiliary Ferrying Squadron

On September 5, the Women's Auxiliary Ferrying Squadron (WAFS) was activated with twenty-eight-year-old Nancy Harkness Love as director. She immediately sent telegrams to eighty-three experienced female pilots. On September 10, Secretary of War Henry Stimson publicly announced the program. Women who had not received telegrams responded when newspaper and magazine articles reported that women pilots were being recruited to serve their country.

At about the same time, Jacqueline Cochran was named director of a training program for women pilots, called the Women's Flying Training Detachment (WFTD). The WFTD was separate from the WAFS. Women pilots with many hours of experience would fill the first WAFS squadron, but more pilots would be needed. The WFTD would train those pilots.

Nancy Harkness Love (*third from right*) and commanding officer Colonel Robert H. Baker (*far right*) inspect the first group of WAFS pilots in September 1942.

On October 19, 1942, seven women from the WAFS, in addition to Love, completed the training program and could start ferrying planes. On October 22, six of the new graduates received their first ferrying assignment. They were to deliver Piper Cubs from the factory in Lock Haven, Pennsylvania, to Mitchel Field on Long Island, New York.

Love wanted to prove that women could fly the new, bigger airplanes. What better way to do this than to fly the planes herself? She had her sights set on the P-51 Mustang, one of the fastest airplanes ever built. Because her first flight in the P-51 would be solo, she would need to rely on her own past experience and her instincts. She taxied down the runway and felt the plane lift off the ground. She soared 10,000 feet (3,048 meters) in this plane. Yes, she could handle this plane. Her WAFS could, too.

By December 1942, the army's ferrying demands had increased. Pilots were needed to fly bigger, faster, and heavier planes. A single squadron of women pilots in Delaware was no longer sufficient. Love knew that additional WAFS units should be formed at other bases.

She traveled the country, evaluating other bases where male ferrying squadrons were located. She chose Dallas, Texas; Romulus, Michigan, outside Detroit; and Long Beach, California. During the first six months of 1943, she "checked out" (flew successfully) in cargo planes, bombers, and attack planes. Then she got a call from Colonel Tunner at Ferrying Division Headquarters in Cincinnati, Ohio. He wanted her back at headquarters.

The Women Airforce Service Pilots

The summer of 1943 would be a "hot" one. Jacqueline Cochran continued to fight for control of all women pilots, not just the Women's Flying Training Detachment. In July, her office moved from Fort Worth, Texas, to the Pentagon in Washington, DC. She was named director of women pilots with the Army Air Force. In August, the Ferrying Division announced that all women pilots would serve under a new organization—Women Airforce Service Pilots (WASP)—and that Jacqueline Cochran would be its director. At the same time, Love was appointed executive in the Air Transport Command for WASP.

Colonel Tunner continued to support Love and her ferrying squadron of women pilots. He called her into his office and offered her the chance to fly a B-17, called "the Flying Fortress," to England. Until then, women pilots had been restricted to domestic flights, within the borders of the United States. To prepare for the flight, she would need advanced training, including night flying, night landing, and instrument operations. Betty Gillies, an original member of the WAFS, was also part of the training. She would be copilot.

The International Flight

On September 2, Love and Gillies began their trip. They flew from Cincinnati to Presque Isle in Maine. On September 3, 1943, they landed in Goose Bay, Labrador, Canada, planning to leave for Prestwick, Scotland, the next day. Unfortunately, General Hap Arnold learned of the mission, and Love and Gillies were grounded. General Arnold ordered their plane reassigned to a male pilot. He was afraid of the publicity that would result if women pilots were killed in a war zone.

Love and Gillies returned to domestic ferrying missions. By October 1944, 130 women pilots ferried two-thirds of all pursuit aircraft manufactured in the United States. They flew the planes from their factories to the airfields from which they would leave for locations overseas. The women were surprised and hurt, then, when General Arnold announced that WASP would be deactivated. Love had heard talk of deactivation but believed that her ferrying squadrons would be protected.

Love's hopes were dashed, however. The letter delivered in October was sent to all WASP, including those in the ATC's ferrying group. Between October and December 20, the date of deactivation, the women pilots took Love's advice to try flying all of the planes available, even the larger ones. They flew any kind of airplane they could get their hands on, until finally, on December 19, thirty-eight WASP gathered in Wilmington, Delaware, one last time. They toasted each other's accomplishments at the Officer's Club. Then they returned to their barracks to pack for the trip home.

Betty Gillies poses with a new sport plane at an aviation show in April 1933. Gillies was one of the first members of the WAFS and was Love's copilot on the first international ferrying flight undertaken by women pilots.

After WASP

Love felt betrayed by the deactivation of WASP, but her flying days were not yet over. Colonel Tunner, who had supported her from the beginning of the WAFS, had been transferred to Calcutta, India. He commanded the ferrying division that supplied the Chinese army's fight against Japan by flying over the Himalayas and the jungles of Burma. Tunner asked that Love be assigned to his division. Her work was largely administrative, interviewing pilots and staff. She took side trips to China and the Assam Valley in India and returned home in January 1945. In 1946, she was awarded the Air Medal by General Harold George and a citation signed by President Harry Truman.

After the war, Love had three daughters and helped her husband with his airplane and boating business. In 1952, she and her family moved to Martha's Vineyard, an island off the coast of Massachusetts. She continued to fly, taking her daughters to doctor and dentist appointments by air. She died at age sixty-two on October 22, 1976, one year, one month, and one day before the bill giving

Love adjusts her helmet before taking off on a ferrying mission. After the WASP program was shut down, Love continued to work for the military in Asia under the command of Colonel William Tunner.

veteran's status to the WASP would be signed by President Jimmy Carter.

The first women accepted into the WASP knew that more than their own success was at stake. Most people, even other women, believed that "girls" were too small and frail to handle the controls of a combat airplane. If this group of women pilots failed, they failed as women, not as individuals. The struggle to be accepted for their talent and ability rather than dismissed because of their gender would continue for decades. Claire Booth Luce, on being appointed United States ambassador to Italy by President Dwight D. Eisenhower in 1953, said, "Because I am a woman, I must make unusual efforts to succeed. If I fail, no one will say, 'She doesn't have what it takes,' They will say, 'Women don't have what it takes.'"

Jackie Cochran's Difficult Road to Success

Jacqueline "Jackie" Cochran was one of the most important figures in the formation of the Women's Auxiliary Army Corps and the Women Airforce Service Pilots. Outside of her wartime activities, Cochran was a well-known racing pilot and the first woman to break the sound barrier. She began her flying career in 1932 and quickly achieved her pilot's license. Three years later, she founded her own cosmetics company and used her aviation skills to promote her products.

When World War II began in Europe, Cochran, like Nancy Harkness Love, helped ferry aircraft from American factories to British bases. Unlike Love, Cochran actually engaged directly in the war effort in Europe by working with the British air force. Cochran eventually became the head of the Women Airforce Service Pilots, with Love as the leader of the ferrying division. By all accounts, Cochran was an impressive aviator whose work during the war was invaluable to air force leaders.

A Self-Made Woman

Jackie Cochran always said that she was an orphan who had grown up in an extremely impoverished foster family in Florida and who had worked a series of odd jobs in order to escape her difficult situation. In fact, she grew up with loving parents who were poor but never lacked for food or other basic necessities. Her given name was Bessie Lee Pittman, but she changed her last name to "Cochran" when she married Robert Cochran, an aircraft mechanic, in her mid-teens. They had a child together who sadly passed away, and Robert either left her or was killed in an auto accident when Cochran was around twenty years old.

Cochran had trained as a beautician and soon became a partner in a beauty shop in Pensacola, Florida. Within just a few years, though, she was ready for bigger things. In her mid-twenties, Cochran sold her share of the shop to her partner, moved to New York City, and changed her name to Jacqueline. Jackie Cochran soon found a job at celebrated hairdresser Antoine Cierplikowski's salon in Saks Fifth Avenue. Cierplikowski's clients included Coco Chanel, actress Greta Garbo, and even First Lady Eleanor Roosevelt.

Cierplikowski also had a salon in Miami, and soon Cochran found herself spending the winter months there. In 1932, at a dinner party in a Miami hotel, she met Floyd Odlum, who at age thirty-six had become a self-made millionaire. She told him that she had been considering starting her own business, a company selling cosmetics. She thought it would give her a chance to travel. Odlum gave her advice that changed her life. He suggested that she could reach more customers if she learned to fly an airplane. Floyd Odlum's relationship with Cochran did not end with that advice. He also would become her husband on May 10, 1936.

Hairdresser Antoine Cierplikowski stands behind a client. Cierplikowski, known as Antoine de Paris, helped popularize the bob haircut in the early twentieth century.

Once Cochran had her pilot's license, she was not content to use it simply to sell cosmetics. In 1937, after Amelia Earhart had disappeared, Cochran entered the Bendix International Air Race. She won the women's purse and finished third, ahead of most male competitors. She continued to race, setting speed records. On December 4, 1937, she raced from New York to Miami in four hours and twelve minutes, setting a national record.

Flying with the ATA

In September 1939, Poland surrendered to the German army. Jackie Cochran wrote a letter to First Lady Eleanor

Amelia Earhart

One of the most famous female aviators in American history, Amelia Earhart was born in Kansas to Edwin, a lawyer, and Amy Earhart. Amy Earhart encouraged Amelia and Amelia's little sister, Grace, to be more outspoken and independent than little girls were usually allowed to be. Both girls grew up wearing bloomers rather than dresses, and they were allowed to run free around their neighborhood, climbing trees and exploring the area. In 1921, at the age of twenty-three, Earhart took her first flying lesson with aviation pioneer Anita Snook. In 1932, inspired by Charles Lindbergh's 1927 flight alone from New York to France, Earhart became the first woman to fly nonstop solo across the Atlantic Ocean. She continued to set records for solo flights and participated in long-distance races. In 1937, Earhart attempted a solo flight around the world. She disappeared over the Pacific Ocean in July 1937. Her body was never found.

An inspiration for generations of pilots, Amelia Earhart became the first woman to fly solo across the Atlantic Ocean in 1932. Earhart disappeared in 1937 during an attempt to fly around the world.

Roosevelt, suggesting that women pilots could play an important role in the military, flying noncombat missions. Cochran was available to begin the necessary planning. The Army Air Corps, however, was not ready to send women into the air.

In March 1941, the United States was still officially neutral, not an active participant, in the war in Europe. President Franklin D. Roosevelt, however, found a way to help Great Britain. He asked Congress to pass the Lend-Lease Act, which allowed the United States to "lend" supplies, like tanks and airplanes, to the Allied forces. American pilots flew planes to Canada. The British Air Transport Auxiliary (ATA) had the responsibility of getting the planes to England.

At an awards luncheon, Cochran discussed the British ATA's problem with General Hap Arnold of the US Army Air Corps and Clayton Knight, who directed the American recruiting effort. They were desperate for pilots, so much so that British women were already serving as pilots for the British air force. General Arnold suggested that Cochran contact ATA headquarters in Montreal and volunteer her services.

Cochran was thrilled to have a chance to participate in the war effort. In June, she completed her flight test in Montreal and was ordered to ferry a Lockheed Hudson from Montreal to Prestwick, Scotland. However, the ATA pilots in Montreal objected because they worried that the ATA would be blamed for her possible death. As a compromise, ATA command decided that Cochran's male copilot would handle the takeoff and landing. She would pilot the plane across the Atlantic. On June 17, Cochran and her crew took off from Montreal. Twelve hours later, they landed in Scotland.

Cochran did not just make the flight to deliver her plane. She also wanted to see how the British ATA worked. In July 1941, she became a tactical consultant, working with Colonel Robert Olds. Cochran and her staff of seven researchers checked three hundred thousand files at the Civil Aeronautics Administration (CAA). They found 2,733 female licensed pilots, 150 with more than 200 hours of flying experience, enough to qualify as commercial airline pilots. Cochran sent them all a questionnaire asking if they would be willing to fly for their country during a war. More than 130 pilots responded. Yes, they were ready.

The Women's Flying Training Detachment

In July 1941, Cochran submitted a proposal to General Hap Arnold for an "Organization of a Woman Pilot's Division of the Air Corps Ferrying Command." Like Love's similar suggestion to Robert Olds, this proposal was discarded as unnecessary, since General Arnold did not see a reason to use female pilots because there were enough male pilots still available. Arnold spoke to Cochran and suggested that she accept the British ATA's request to recruit female pilots for duty overseas.

Cochran accepted that challenge, promising the ATA to recruit 125 female pilots with three hundred hours of flying experience. She had a difficult time. The female pilots were required to commit to an eighteen-month overseas contract. Some had families with small children and were unwilling to leave them behind. Many believed that if the British used female pilots, then eventually the American government would, too, so they saw no reason to go to Britain when

General Henry H. "Hap" Arnold was chief of the Army Air Corps from 1938 to 1941. Born in 1886, Arnold was trained to fly by the Wright brothers and became one of the first ever military pilots.

they might eventually serve the same role in America. Cochran had to assure her ATA recruits that the US military had refused her proposal and had no intention of using female pilots in the near future. General Arnold directed the Ferry Command not to hire female pilots until Cochran had fulfilled her agreement with the British.

Then, on December 7, 1941, the Japanese attacked Pearl Harbor. World War II was no longer the European War—the United States was now heavily involved. President Roosevelt declared war on Japan. On December 11, he declared war on Germany and Italy. Suddenly, the need for American combat pilots became critical, and as male pilots were pulled to the front lines, their civilian duties were taken over by female aviators. Cochran's goals of leading female pilots in wartime would eventually come to fruition—but not without some obstacles along the way.

3

Working as a Part of WASP

In the spring of 1942, Cochran went to England to oversee the arrival of the first group of the twenty-five American female pilots she had recruited for the ATA. By late August, the last recruits would be sworn into service. General Arnold visited Cochran in London. He told her that soon female pilots would also be needed in the United States. He would soon need her back to take on this task.

While Cochran was in England, however, Nancy Harkness Love spoke with Colonel William Tunner and General Harold George. Without discussing the plans with General Arnold, on September 10, Secretary of War Henry L. Stimson announced the formation of the Women's Auxiliary Ferrying Squadron, with Love as director. Cochran was furious and, on her return from England, stormed into General Arnold's office to advocate for herself. She argued that she, not Love, should be the one leading those women.

Cochran got her wish, after a while. On September 15, 1942, the War Department announced the formation of a second group of female pilots, a training group. This second program, to be directed by Jacqueline Cochran, was called the Women's Flying Training Detachment (WFTD). A month later, the United States Army Air Force publicly announced the start of this training program, and Jackie Cochran was flooded with at least twenty-five thousand applications. She and three assistants traveled around the country, giving interviews, arranging medical

Jacqueline Cochran (*center*) visits a Royal Air Force (RAF) station in the United Kingdom in 1941. Before the United States entered World War II, Cochran volunteered with the RAF as a pilot with the Air Transport Auxiliary (ATA).

41

examinations, and making final decisions. Out of the twenty-five thousand, Cochran planned to train about one thousand pilots.

A Rough Beginning

To get her first training class in the air, Cochran needed a base from which to operate. In November, she chose Aviation Enterprises, Ltd., located at Howard Hughes Field at Houston Municipal Airport in Texas. Rooms in local tourist motels served as housing. The trainees traveled from the motels to the airfield in army supply semitrailer trucks. The women sat on wooden boards built into the backs of the trucks.

What to Wear?

One major difficulty the WFTD faced was clothing. The trainees had not been promised uniforms and instead had to buy their own clothes. When a pile of GI flying suits finally arrived in mid-December, the trainees were thrilled, but their joy was short-lived. The khaki GI jumpsuits were men's sizes. The shoulders and pant legs were so large that the women nicknamed them "zoot suits." To wear the suits, the women had to roll up the sleeves and pant legs and tie a belt around the waist. Later on, at the first graduation of the WASP members, the female pilots were dressed in khaki pants and blouses they had bought themselves. General Arnold, also present at the ceremony, suggested to Cochran that the "girls" deserved uniforms. Cochran agreed. She went to Bergdorf Goodman's in New York City and paid to have a uniform designed. The "Santiago Blue" suits were stylish, sophisticated, and professional.

Leonora Horton and Mildred Axton wear "zoot suits," the WASP trainees' nickname for the too-large flight suits they were sent to wear as uniforms.

The biggest problem was finding airplanes for the women to fly. Army trainer aircraft were on order but had not yet arrived. Cochran and the training command took control of almost every private plane between Fort Worth and Houston.

Cochran was not happy with the Houston airfield. She wanted a location that could be developed into a permanent training center, handling classes of more than 125 pilots. The British were giving up their base in Sweetwater, Texas. Cochran arranged to take it over, naming her new base Avenger Field. In March 1943, she instructed the Houston trainees to pack their belongings and ferry themselves and their airplanes to Sweetwater.

The new facility was not fancy, but it was an improvement over Houston. Eight huts served as barracks. They were divided into six-woman bunkrooms called bays. A longer building housed classrooms and the "ready room," where pilots waited their turn to fly. Each day, half the trainees were in class; the rest were in the air or waiting to fly. A control tower and a hangar were under construction.

In August 1943, the WFTD and the WAFS merged to become WASP, with Cochran as the head. Cochran felt that her biggest responsibility as the WASP leader was to get military status for the WASP. Initially, the Army Air Force assumed that WASP would become part of the Women's Army Corps (WAC, formerly called the WAAC), which was already militarized. Cochran, however, knew that if her pilots were WACs, she would lose control of her program.

Petitioning for Military Status

Cochran hoped Congress would pass a bill giving the WASP corps military status. On February 19, 1944, the bill was introduced. The opposition, however, was prepared for this, and public opinion was generally against the bill. The Civilian Pilot Training Program had already been shut down, leaving its male instructors without flying jobs. Also, at this time, many people still believed that women belonged at home. Female pilots had been helpful for a time, filling in for men who were not available. However, now that men were ready to take over, many believed the women should willingly give up their seats in the cockpits. Numerous articles in newspapers and magazines supported this view. Public support of WASP was overwhelmed by rumors that female pilots did not really care about serving their country and that they only wanted to keep flying because they found it glamorous. Although these claims were untrue, the prevailing attitudes of the time made people more likely to believe negative things written about the female pilots than any arguments in favor of them being granted mililtary status and seen in the same light as male pilots.

The Deactivation of WASP

Of course, flying for the military was not really glamorous. It was dangerous, hard, sweaty work. But people did not understand this because WASP had been kept isolated. Most Americans had not even known the program existed. Cochran had never tried to gain public support for her program. Letters opposing WASP militarization flooded Congress. Cochran, however, refused to allow any member of the WASP to write to her senator or representative. She

Jackie Cochran sits in a Royal Canadian Air Force fighter jet, the same kind of aircraft she used when she became the first woman to break the sound barrier in 1953.

also forbade any WASP member to go to Washington. Some family members wrote on behalf of the WASP, but their words were not enough. On June 21, 1944, Congress defeated the bill to militarize WASP.

The defeat of militarization did not eliminate the WASP program. Public opposition to the program was growing. Cochran prepared an extensive public report outlining the accomplishments of WASP. Although the press reported the information, detailing how the female pilots were serving the war efforts, Cochran was fighting a losing battle.

In October, 1944, WASP members across the country received letters announcing their deactivation on December 20. Jacqueline Cochran, however, would not be deactivated. She continued to fly, setting records and receiving awards. In 1953, she became the first woman to break the sound barrier, and in 1971, she became the first living woman enshrined in the National Aviation Hall of Fame. Cochran died in 1980 at her home in California at the age of seventy-four.

4

Aircraft Tester Evelyn Sharp

Jack Jefford is best known as the husband of famed Alaskan air taxi pilot and violinist Ruth Jefford, but in 1935, well before he met Ruth, Jefford decided to create a flying school in the small town of Ord, Nebraska. At the time, Jefford rented rooms at a boardinghouse owned by a man named John Sharp. It was the height of the Great Depression, so it was perhaps unsurprising that Jefford quickly ran out of funds; few people could afford the luxury of flying lessons, which made it difficult for Jefford to pay for his room and board. Sharp didn't want to kick the man out, so they came to an agreement: Jefford would work off his debt by teaching Sharp's teenage daughter, Evelyn, to fly.

Without realizing it, John Sharp had changed the direction of his daughter's life forever. Soon, Evelyn Sharp would become a celebrity, earning her living and supporting the Sharp family as a flight instructor and barnstormer. She was one of the first female airmail pilots and trained over 350 men in piloting aircraft. Later on, she would serve her country as one of the youngest members of the Women's Auxiliary Ferrying Squadron (WAFS).

Ruth Jefford, months before her death in January 2007, holds the Wright Brothers Master Pilot Award, which she received in September 2006.

The Making of Evelyn Sharp

The circumstances of Sharp's early life make her rise to celebrity even more surprising. She was born in Melstone, Montana, on October 20, 1919, to Orla and Elsie Crouse. Their wedding had been arranged quickly when they discovered that Elsie was pregnant. The marriage soon ended in divorce, leaving Elsie with a difficult choice. She would be unable to care for a baby alone. She arranged for John and Mary Sharp to adopt her baby. On December 2, 1919, Evelyn Genevieve Sharp became the legal daughter of John and Mary Sharp, moving with them to Kinsey, Montana.

When she was three years old, Evelyn and her family moved to Nebraska. Like most families during the Depression, John and Mary Sharp worked hard and suffered financial setbacks. They operated a grocery store and boardinghouse. They tried their hand at farming outside of Hastings, Nebraska. When the farm failed, the Sharps moved to Ord.

On February 4, 1935, Jack Jefford made the first payment on his debt to John Sharp. Evelyn had her flying lesson. On November 9, 1936, she passed her flight test, becoming a licensed private pilot. She was able to fly any single-engine airplane and take passengers for pleasure.

Just as her career appeared to be taking off, Sharp found herself grounded. Jack Jefford had closed his flying school and moved to Hastings. John Sharp, however, found a way for his daughter to fly. He convinced local businessmen to sponsor her, and togther the men purchased a plane for Sharp to fly. She became a celebrity, bringing publicity to Ord, and soon she was able to generate income by charging for rides.

Amelia Earhart boards a single-engine aircraft, like the ones Evelyn Sharp learned to fly while training with Jefford. Light and maneuverable, single-engine airplanes are still in use today as private planes and stunt vehicles.

Putting Flying Skills to Good Use

Sharp finally was able to support herself and her family doing what she loved. She crisscrossed the country, giving flight demonstrations, barnstorming shows, and pleasure rides. At the same time, the mood in the country was changing. The war in Europe was on everyone's mind. Sharp wanted to use her flying skills to help. In June 1940, she moved to Spearfish, North Dakota, to be an instructor for the Civilian Pilot Training Program (CPTP). She taught for the CPTP until December, and then moved to California to work as a flight instructor there.

On September 5, 1942, Sharp was one of eighty-four women who received a telegram inviting them to Wilmington, Delaware, to apply for the Women's Auxiliary Ferrying Squadron. Sharp went to Wilmington, Delaware, where she passed her interview and flight test. She was accepted on October 20, 1942. She moved to New Castle Army Air Base (NCAAB) and into Bachelor's Officer

A Double Standard

To be eligible for WASP, women pilots needed to meet stiffer requirements than male pilots. Men pilots could be between the ages of nineteen and forty-five. Only women ages twenty-one to thirty-five were eligible. Women needed five hundred hours of flying time, men only two hundred. Women needed a high school diploma; men needed to have completed only three years of high school. Men were trained as civilians for ninety days and then were commissioned into the Army Air Force. Women would remain civilians unless Congress passed a new law. Also, women were paid $250 a month; men were paid $380.

Quarters 14 (BOQ 14), which had recently been vacated by its male residents. Teresa James, another WAFS recruit, described the conditions in BOQ 14 in *The Originals: The Woman's Auxiliary Ferrying Squadron of World War II*:

> Our new home was built from two-by-fours, planks and boards. One window per room, two if you had a corner room ... I never expected to see such a barren structure, because I had been informed that the men who had occupied BOQ 14 had moved to another building. I ...was astonished at the sunlight peeking through the cracks in the walls ... I picked out a room with the least daylight peeking through the cracks. Furnishings consisted of one sagging cot and one iron chair.[1]

The building had a common bathroom, but the shower stalls had no curtains, and the toilets were out in the open. Modesty would become a thing of the past. Because many buildings at NCAAB were under construction, the ground was a sea of mud. To avoid sinking to her ankles, Sharp had to walk across planks from the road to the building. During her thirty-day training period, Sharp paid seventy-five cents a day to live in these conditions at BOQ 14.

While training, Sharp spent twenty-five hours flying and seventy-two hours at ground school. By November 1942, she had completed her training and was eligible to wear the WAFS uniform: a belted jacket, matching shirt and slacks, and an overseas cap. Despite their training, the WAFS pilots weren't considered an official part of the military and therefore had to pay for their own conditions. It was neither fair nor right, but the women of the WAFS

WASP trainees walk past aircraft at Lared Army Air Field in January 1944. The WAFS program and Jackie Cochran's Women's Flying Training Detachment (WFTD) merged to form the WASP program.

suffered through these difficult conditions in order to gain the opportunity to fly for their country.

On Assignment with WAFS

Sharp's first assignment as a member of the WAFS was to fly one of ten new PT-19As from their factory in Hagerstown, Maryland, to Riddle-McKay Army Primary School in Union City, Tennessee. She and nine other WAFS rode a train to Maryland where they were stranded for days, waiting for miserable weather to clear. After they safely delivered the planes, their orders were to return as quickly as possible to NCAAB. Unfortunately, they were not allowed to hitch rides on any military planes piloted by men. No hint of scandal could be allowed to tarnish the WAFS reputation. When she returned to Wilmington,

Weather Trouble

During the winter, flights were a bone-chilling event. The PT-19As had open cockpits, so there was no protection from the cold or precipitation. Dressing to survive the freezing wind was the most important preparation. Sharp wore woolen underwear under her uniform, which was made up of a leather-covered, fleece-lined, two-piece garment, and a pair of leather-covered, fleece-lined flying boots weighing about 15 pounds (6.8 kilograms). She added a fleece-lined helmet; a fleece-lined face mask with holes for eyes, nose, and mouth; goggles with fleece around the edges of the eyepiece to protect her face from metal; and fleece-lined flying gloves. In addition, she carried a 25-pound (11 kg) parachute. Her navigational charts had to be strapped to her leg so that they wouldn't blow out of the cockpit.

Sharp was handed a new set of orders. She reported to Lock Haven, Pennsylvania, and flew from there to Fort Smith, Arkansas. This would become the pattern of her early life with the WAFS: a train ride to pick up the plane; the delivery flight, weather permitting; and a train or bus ride back to base.

By early 1943, the twenty-eight original members of the WAFS had finished training. They were divided among four locations and were eventually joined by women graduating from Jacqueline Cochran's WFTD program. Sharp was assigned to Long Beach Army Air Base in California. Soon after she arrived, restrictions that had kept women from flying larger, heavier planes were lifted. Sharp would be able to fly twin-engine cargo planes and pursuit aircraft, cruising at about 250 miles per hour (450 kmh).

At the end of September, Sharp was transferred to Palm Springs, California, where she became commander of the Twenty-First Squadron. Suddenly, in November, she was transferred back to Long Beach. Palm Springs had been designated a pursuit training school, but she was not chosen for the first class.

Bigger and Better Aircraft

Back at Long Beach, Sharp began training for instrument flying. She wanted to fly more sophisticated aircraft and would need to be able to navigate without using landmarks on the ground. At Long Beach, a Link Trainer, a simulator, allowed pilots to practice instrument "flying" without leaving the ground and risking the danger of getting lost or crashing. As she felt more comfortable, Sharp also practiced in real flight. She passed the first of

" CURTISS P-40 " PU

The aircraft in this image are Curtiss P-40 Warhawks, a model that was introduced in 1938 and used by the air forces of most of the Allies during World War II.

three instrument flight checks in January 1944 and the last on March 29, 1944.

The next day, she climbed into a "Lightning" P-38J destined for Newark, New Jersey. Fog forced her down in Palm Springs, where she spent the night. On March 31, she flew across Arizona and New Mexico to Amarillo, Texas. On April 1, she flew all the way to Harrisburg, Pennsylvania, refueling in Oklahoma, Illinois, and Ohio on the way. The weather changed for the worse, and on April 2, she was able to fly only a short distance to New Cumberland, Pennsylvania.

The next morning, Sharp taxied down the runway and lifted off for what would become her final flight. The Lightning had a reputation for losing an engine on takeoff—a pilot's worst nightmare. Unfortunately, Sharp's nightmare came true. The ground crew saw smoke pouring from her left engine. She barely had enough height to avoid hitting the tower. Most likely, Sharp knew she was in trouble. She altered her course to avoid crashing in a residential area. Soon after takeoff, the plane crashed in a "pancake landing." Although the plane did not dive into the ground, the impact drove the front (nose) wheel up through the cockpit. The force broke the straps of Sharp's harness and sent her bursting through the canopy. She died instantly.

Sharp's Legacy

Because the WAFS had never been made part of the military, Sharp's family received no death benefits. Nancy Harkness Love asked another member of the WAFS, Nancy Batson, to accompany Sharp's body from Harrisburg

Born in February 1920, Nancy Batson was one of the first women enrolled in the WAFS program. Batson continued to fly after the war and even founded a flying business.

back to Ord, Nebraska. With her, Batson carried $200 collected from fellow WAFS to give to Sharp's family.

It seemed that the whole town of Ord turned out for Sharp's funeral on Easter Sunday, April 9, 1944. One man, his eyes brimming with tears, asked Batson if he could drape Sharp's casket with an American flag. She agreed. The citizens of Ord would not let Sharp's sacrifice go unnoticed. On September 12, 1948, thousands of people came to honor her at the dedication of Ord Municipal Airport as Evelyn Sharp Field. A monument holding a three-bladed propeller from a P-38 stood over a concrete pyramid holding memorabilia from Sharp's flying career. During the ceremony, members of the Nebraska Air National Guard flew overhead.

In June 1996, the first annual Evelyn Sharp Day was held in Ord. The Nebraska State Historical Society displays a collection commemorating her achievements, and she is honored as a member of Nebraska's Aviation Hall of Fame. In 2018, a memorial dedicated to Sharp was unveiled at the site of the crash at the Pfeiffer Memorial Arboretum and Nature Preserve in Cumberland County, Pennsylvania.

5

Dot Swain, the Artist Aviator

Across the country, bronze statues of a young woman in a flight suit, *The WASP Trainee*, stand at different World War II memorial spaces, including Sweetwater, Texas, the original home of the WASP program. Another stands at the United States Air Force Academy, a reminder of the first women to fly for the United States military. The artist who sculpted *The WASP Trainee* was a WASP herself: Dorothy "Dot" Swain Lewis was an instructor and pilot in the WASP program. One of just ten women chosen by the famous aviator Phoebe Omlie in 1942 to be trained as a flight instructor, Swain taught WASP trainees and flew military aircraft. After the war, she became a flight instructor in Florida and has been recognized as a pioneer in aviation and for her service with the WASP.

Early Life in Asheville

Dot Swain was born in 1915 in Asheville, North Carolina. She was the second of four children born to Mozelle Stringfield Swain and John Edward Swain. Her mother, a gifted musician, taught Swain and her siblings to love music and art. After high school, Swain was admitted to Randolph-Macon Women's College in Lynchburg, Virginia.

An aircraft sculpture is found outside the United States Air Force Academy Chapel. The Air Force Academy is located in Colorado and, like the other four American service academies, is highly selective.

SPONSORS

EIGHTH AIR FORCE UNITED STATES ARMY AIR FORCES

After graduation, she decided to move to the major center for the arts—New York City.

In January 1937, Swain began taking art classes. She planned to become a professional artist, creating illustrations for magazines and newspapers. Then, one summer afternoon in June 1940, while driving to her family's home in Asheville, Swain noticed a small yellow single-engine plane flying overhead. She stopped at the Asheville-Hendersonville Airport and paid $4 for a half-hour flight. After that, she was hooked. She wanted not simply to ride as a passenger, but to fly the plane herself.

She decided to take flying lessons, and soon those Saturday morning lessons were the highlight of her week. In August 1940, Swain soloed for the first time, completing eight hours of flight time. She borrowed $150 from her sister, Betty, to pay for more flying lessons. During the summer of 1941, she flew nearly every day, accumulating forty-seven hours. In October, she passed the tests for becoming a private pilot.

Training at the Women's Research Flight Instructor School

Swain had planned to be an illustrator. Flying was still a hobby. But the Japanese attack on Pearl Harbor on December 7, 1941, changed the lives of all Americans. Suddenly, resources were scarce. Newspapers had trouble finding paper on which to print. The prospects for a young illustrator trying to break into the business were poor at best. Swain began to think her flying ability might be of use in the country's war effort and got a job with Piper Aircraft Company in Lock Haven, Pennsylvania, in March 1942. Her job was to make airplane parts and to deliver Piper

Cub planes for the factory. By the end of the summer of 1942, she had logged more than 250 hours of flying time.

In September 1942, Swain's flying career took a new direction. She received a notice from Phoebe Omlie, who invited Swain to apply for the first women's aviation instruction program. Omlie had convinced the secretary of commerce that female flight instructors could train college students and military pilots, and thus began the Women's Research Flight Instructor School. Swain was just one of ten women Omlie had picked for the program. She decided to accept the offer and made her way to Gillespie Airfield in Nashville, Tennessee.

Empowerment and Sexuality

The history of homosexuality and the military is complicated, but in many ways, the Women's Army Corps (WAC) provided a somewhat safe space for lesbians to find a community of other lesbian women. The WAC began as the Women's Auxiliary Army Corps in 1942, but by 1943, the WAC was converted to active military status and dropped the "Auxiliary" part of the name. Although homosexuality was technically not allowed in the military, many of the regulations against it targeted gay men; because women had only recently been allowed to join the military, and because of certain cultural ideas about femininity, lesbians had a comparatively easier time flying under the radar. They also benefited from the new roles women took on during World War II. Because so many men were off at war, women were encouraged to both work and socialize more outside the home, including going out to lesbian bars.

Attorney General Janet Reno (*left*) uncovers her official portrait in January 2001 alongside Dorothy Swain Lewis (*right*), who painted the portrait.

Swain passed her flight check easily, but the course was grueling. Beginning at 6:45 a.m., trainees were kept busy with physical training, ground school courses, and flight instruction. By bedtime, they were exhausted. To pass the course, Swain needed 43 hours of flight instruction, 18 hours of solo flying, 216 hours of ground training, 18 hours of physical training, 36 hours of ground school instruction training, and 162 hours of training in aviation mechanics. She graduated from the course in February 1943 and was sent to Portales, New Mexico, to teach navy seamen to fly.

Swain's students in New Mexico were beginning flyers with little training. Eventually, the airmen who completed all their training would be flying off of aircraft carriers. She taught four classes, stressing the "circle to the spot" landings that would enable her students to get their planes down safely on the deck of an aircraft carrier. Swain enjoyed teaching her eager airmen, but she yearned to leave her little two-seater behind and pilot sleek, powerful military planes. She wanted to join WASP.

Ye Olde Fox Hutch

She requested an exchange from the navy program and in June 1943 became an instructor for the women's military training program, arriving in Sweetwater, Texas, for Class 43-W-8. She shared a tiny house with four other instructors. Technically, the instructors' house, nicknamed "Ye Olde Fox Hutch," was off-limits to WASP trainees. The penalties for social interaction between students and instructors had been designed when all the instructors were men to prevent romantic relationships from developing.

Swain and her roommates provided one of the few social alternatives to life in the barracks.

In August 1943, WASP trainees ring the fire bell after completing their ground school and basic flight training programs.

A-36 502

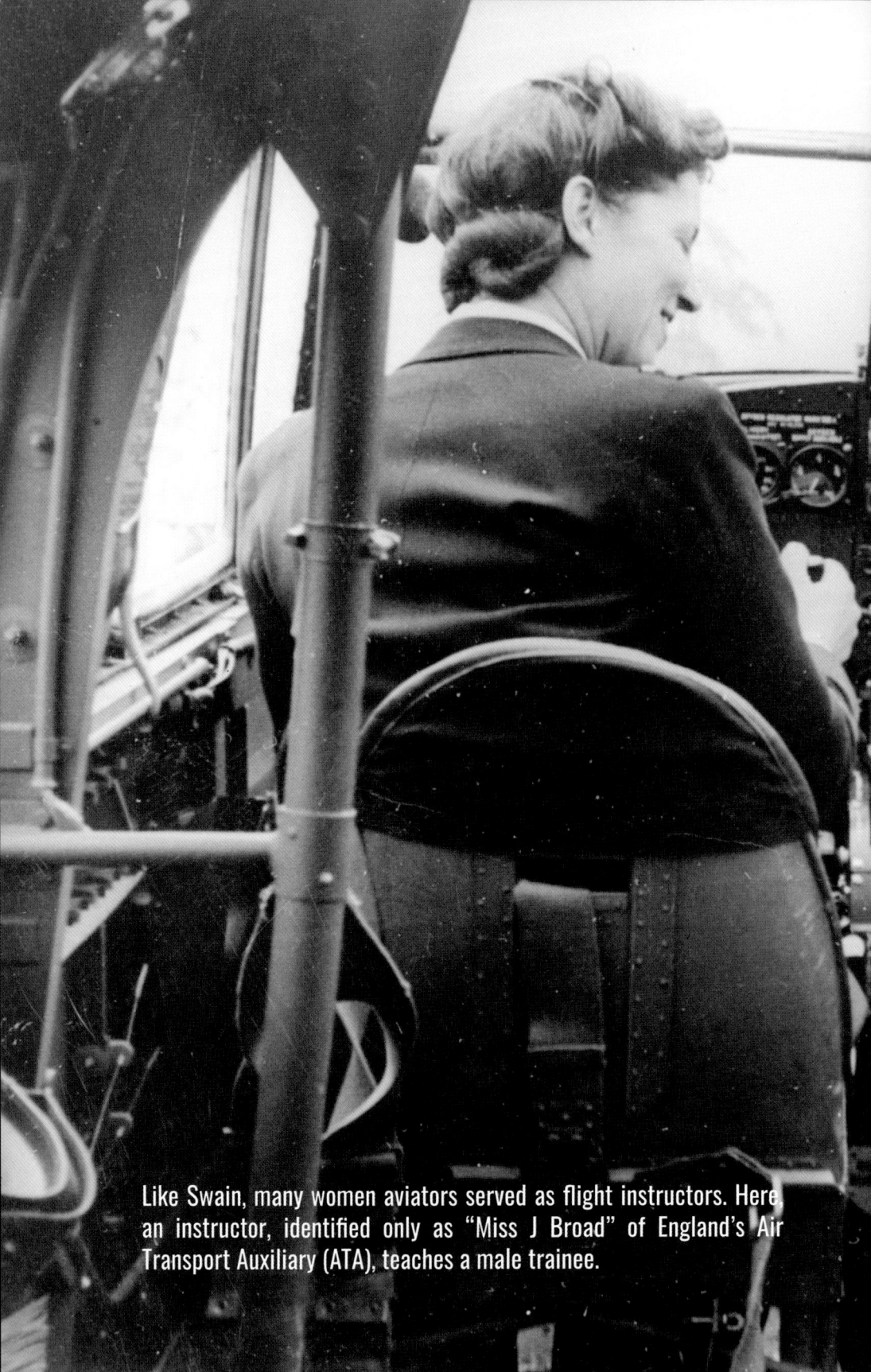

Like Swain, many women aviators served as flight instructors. Here, an instructor, identified only as "Miss J Broad" of England's Air Transport Auxiliary (ATA), teaches a male trainee.

Because of this, trainees were willing to risk punishment. Swain's friend and trainee Winifred Wood described a night at Ye Olde Fox Hutch in her book *We Were WASPS*:

> There was always a good hot discussion going on over a few short ones. Someone would drag in a steak and the makings. After Jerry finished the dishes, a task which always seemed to fall to her, Dot would drag out the "git fiddle" [guitar] and entertain us with "Minnie from Trinidad," "Cocaine Bill and Morphine Sue," and others from her large repertoire.[1]

For the trainees, evenings with Swain and her roommates were filled with good music, good food, and fun.

Training in Texas

Although Swain enjoyed her privileges as an instructor, she wanted to learn to fly the newer, more exciting planes. She resigned as a flight instructor, moved into the barracks, and became a WASP trainee. Because of her training as an instructor, she skipped ahead to Class 44-W-5, which had finished its primary flight instruction, for advanced techniques. She graduated on June 27, 1944, and was sent to twin-engine training in Columbus, Missouri, where she flew engineering flight tests on the AT-10.

Then she went to Laredo, Texas, to train as a copilot of the twin-engine Martin B-26. She remained in Laredo, towing targets for gunnery practice. Like Ann Baumgartner, Swain flew her planes to allow soldiers on the ground to practice firing live ammunition. The soldiers did not shoot directly at the planes but aimed at tow flags that were attached to the tail of a plane by a strong cable. In *How High She Flies,* Swain described these maneuvers:

> When I flew the B-26 Martin Marauder, we towed targets for B-24 gunners. We generally planned to meet at 6,000 feet [1,829 m], or 10,000 feet [3,048 m], a predetermined altitude. We'd rendezvous with a B-26 pilot, who would join up above us. We slowed down and released a target on a cable about 400 feet [122 m] behind our aircraft. The gunners shot at those targets. The dangers, actually, weren't from wild gunners, but from the risk of mid-air collision with other B-26s.[2]

Swain stayed on duty at Laredo Air Force Base until December 20, 1944, when the WASPs were disbanded. Suddenly, like the other WASPs around the country, she found she was no longer needed. She went back to Asheville to spend the holidays with her family and begin once again to concentrate on her art career. She received a call from Winifred Wood. Wood planned to write a book about the WASP and asked Swain to do the illustrations. Swain agreed and moved to Florida in January 1945 to work on the cartoons for the book *We Were WASPS.*

Between Arts and Aviation

In August, Swain decided that she needed to pursue her own career. She moved once again to New York City. She found a basement apartment in Greenwich Village and began painting and illustrating greeting cards. It seemed, though, that her life was not yet ready to settle. She went to her first WASP reunion at the Piper Aircraft Company, her past employer, in Lock Haven, Pennsylvania. William T. Piper arranged for one hundred new planes to be held so that the feamle pilots could deliver them, first to the Cleveland National Championship air races and then to their final destinations. When Swain delivered her plane to Red Kurvin in Daytona Beach, Florida, Kurvin immediately offered her a job as an instructor in his new flight school.

Swain also began performing in an air show. Concealed in the audience as a spectator, she would emerge as "Miss Ophelia Pratt," a schoolteacher who had taught herself to milk cows by reading a book. Miss Ophelia was sure that she could teach herself to fly the same way. After a deliberately shaky takeoff, Swain put her plane through a series of acrobatics, demonstrating that anyone can learn to fly. Anyone, that is, with more than 2,500 hours of experience.

Later Life as an Artist and Instructor

As a flight instructor, Swain had many students thanks to the GI Bill, a government program designed to help returning soldiers receive education and training. The bill enabled many men to enroll in flight schools. Albert Zelius "Bert" Lewis, one of those soldiers, became Swain's student. After receiving his license, Lewis and Swain began dating and were married in June 1947. A year later, their son, Albert Jr., was born. Unfortunately, after only two years of marriage, Swain and Lewis divorced. Once again, Swain turned to her love of art. She taught at the Orme School in Arizona from 1951 until 1977.

A gifted sculptor, Swain had created many small statues for WASP. In 1992, she was approached to create a WASP memorial in Sweetwater, Texas. The sculpture stands in the center of the wishing well into which each trainee was plunged after her first successful solo flight. Another statue she made, dedicated in 1997, stands at the courtyard of the United States Air Force Academy in Colorado Springs, Colorado.

In 2009, Swain was granted the Congressional Gold Medal, one of the highest civilian awards in the country, as part of a special ceremony honoring WASP. Later on, Swain moved to California to teach at the Idyllwild School of Music and the Arts. She passed away in California on September 9, 2013, just three weeks shy of her ninety-eighth birthday.

6

The First Woman to Fly a Jet Plane

Ann Baumgartner Carl was a pilot with WASP and the first woman ever to fly an air force jet aircraft. After World War II, Baumgartner became a flight instructor, science journalist, and sailor. Baumgartner grew up in a military family—she was born in Augusta, Georgia, in 1918 at an army hospital while her father was serving in France with the armed forces. When he returned from Europe, the Baumgartners moved to Plainfield, New Jersey.

Baumgartner attended Walnut Hill School in Natick, Massachusetts. At the boarding school, Baumgartner learned to be independent and to think for herself. She was encouraged to challenge herself without limits. She would carry these skills and traits with her through college and into adulthood, and they would serve her well in her career as a pilot and beyond.

War Begins in Europe

After Walnut Hill, Baumgartner became a pre-med major in the class of 1939 at Smith College in Northampton, Massachusetts. As graduation neared, she struggled to decide what to do with her life. She thought that a trip to Europe might help her make a choice. She left on an Italian freighter in the summer of 1939, planning to tour Spain, Sicily, and Italy before meeting her mother in England to stay with family there. On September 1, 1939, while she visited her mother's family, Hitler's armies invaded Poland. Two days later, Britain declared war on Germany.

Her relatives insisted that Baumgartner and her mother leave England as soon as possible. They left on September 2, 1939, on a ship overflowing with refugees. They were packed into a large room where fifty mattresses had been laid on the floor six inches apart. They were unable to change their clothes. The toilet facilities clogged and leaked onto the floor. The fear of being torpedoed and sunk during the voyage hung over the ship. Finally, they steamed past the Statue of Liberty into New York Harbor.

Dreaming of Flying

Back in the United States, Baumgartner found a medical research job in New Jersey, investigating the effects of vitamins that had been extracted from fish oils. At the vitamin company, she sometimes took a break by climbing to the roof for a view of the Manhattan skyline. One evening, she watched an airplane cross the sky. She imagined doing nothing but piloting that airplane across the country, looking at the world stretching away around her. She decided to take flying lessons and become a commercial pilot. Using the money she earned at her research job, she began her flying lessons and soon earned her private pilot's license. She planned to join the Air Transport Auxiliary in England, the only wartime option available to female pilots at the time.

Hoping for an assignment flying an air ambulance, Baumgartner needed to accumulate two hundred hours of flying time, the requirement for a commercial license. She and another pilot, Jasper White, bought an old Piper Cub and alternated flying. She was near her goal in the summer of 1942, when the government, having sighted submarines offshore, closed the eastern coast to all private flying. She feared that her objective would be unreachable. Then she heard a news story about the WFTD. The army was looking for experienced women pilots to fly noncombat missions in the United States. Baumgartner met with Jacqueline Cochran in her Manhattan apartment late in 1942. Shortly before Christmas, Baumgartner received orders to report

England's Air Transport Auxiliary

The Air Transport Auxiliary (ATA) was a civilian organization that ferried aircraft between factories, bases, and other key locations for military use. Initially, the ATA wasn't meant to carry munitions, but demand for pilots in the Royal Air Force was so significant that there were no military pilots left to ferry actual aircraft from place to place, so the ATA took over that responsibility. Because it was a civilian organization, the ATA accepted women as well as men, and by 1943 its female pilots were paid just as much as male pilots. Nicknamed "Attagirls," the first female pilots were accepted into the ATA in 1940, and women from all over Europe and America volunteered with the organization, including Jackie Cochran. Although they couldn't fly on the front lines, the aviators of the ATA played a key role in helping the war effort in Britain.

to Houston, Texas, in January 1943 as part of the WFTD Class of 1943.

As Baumgartner rode the train to Houston, she pictured life on an active air force base with dozens of shining, sleek silver planes lined up along runways busy with incoming and outgoing air traffic. In reality, Jacqueline Cochran had not yet found a permanent home for the first recruits in her program. Anxious to get started, she

ATA women pilots gather in a briefing room in September 1944. Among their other roles, ATA pilots ferried aircraft from the factories where they were made to military bases.

had set up at the end of a runway at the Houston Municipal Airport. There was no mess hall, no barracks, no infirmary—and no bathroom! When necessary, trainees had to walk all the way to the main terminal building. No shiny silver planes shimmered in the sunlight. Instead, Baumgartner only found old Piper Cubs.

Baumgartner and the other recruits were housed in hotels in town, which seemed acceptable until they were assigned to their rooms. Two women were assigned to each room, but the room had only one bed. They would be paid $150 a month and were expected to pay for their own meals. Conditions were poor, but the women

A group of ATA pilots poses in their flight gear. Before the United States joined the war, some Americans flew with the ATA, including Jackie Cochran.

stayed on. They refused to give up this chance to train as pilots for military planes.

Teaching at Camp Davis

Baumgartner took ground school courses, including navigation, meteorology, and Morse code. She learned how an engine works by taking it apart and rebuilding it. Then, one evening, her dream of "real" flight training came true. Air force fighter planes—PT-19s and BT-13s—arrived, sleek and shiny. In the PT-19s, Baumgartner flew cross-country flights, careful to keep the navigation charts from blowing out of the open cockpit. The BT-13 had a canopy over the cockpit and was heavier and more powerful.

Baumgartner spent fifty-five hours in the PT-19 and sixty-five hours in the BT-13. She flew other planes, too, practicing flying with and without instruments. She passed her flight and ground school tests and graduated on September 11, 1943. Her first assignment was to a tow-target squadron of the artillery base at Camp Davis in North Carolina. She would replace a woman who had been killed when her plane crashed.

Baumgartner's mission was to help artillery gunners train. She towed a cloth target behind her airplane. The gunners shot at the target with live ammunition. Although they were not aiming at the planes, many planes returned with bullet holes in them. After all, these men were just learning how to fire their guns. Baumgartner also flew back and forth to test radar tracking by the gunner trainees. She flew at night too. She flew different patterns at varying altitudes while the trainees tried to track her with searchlights. This mission also gave her an opportunity to build up a lot of flying hours. Plus, during her free time, she was encouraged to take cross-country flights to practice her navigational skills.

Testing Equipment at Wright Field

In February 1944, Baumgartner and Betty Greene, another member of WASP, were sent to Wright Field in Dayton, Ohio, to test high-altitude and low-temperature equipment. Wright Field was a research facility where scientists studied the effects of high-altitude flying, oxygen deprivation, and gravitational forces on the human body. Baumgartner and Greene were assigned to participate for about a week. They worked with Dr. Alice Brues to design the best possible flying suit. They wore different clothing so that the results could be compared. They tested clothing for warmth and flexibility. Was an alpaca-lined suit warm enough or too bulky? Should zippers be zipped up or left opened? Would muddy boots slip when pilots climbed on the wing to get into the cockpit? Even underwear and socks were tested.

Once the tests were over, Baumgartner returned to target flying at Camp Davis. Two weeks later, though, she was packing again. In March 1944, her request for a transfer was approved. She was going back to Wright Field as part of the Fighter Flight Test Branch. She was not going to test clothing, though. This time she would be testing the planes.

Usually the purpose of her flight was to test the plane itself or its parts—instruments, engine parts, or overall performance. On one occasion, though, Baumgartner flew a P-51 to test a new gunsight. She flew to a target on the eastern tip of an island in Lake Erie. She made several high-speed passes, shooting the guns at the target.

Since women were not allowed to fly combat missions, Baumgartner was most likely the only WASP to shoot a fighter plane's guns during World War II.

Aircrafts that Made History

Baumgartner not only tested fighter planes, she also tested bombers. Two tests, both involving long-range flights, were especially important. The first was a test to refuel the bomber from another plane in midair, without landing. The

The Lockheed P-80 "Shooting Star" fighter plane was the first fighter jet to be used by the United States military, and Baumgartner was the first woman ever to fly a fighter jet in American history.

second part of the test involved carrying a heavy load for many hours. The load weighed 8,900 pounds (4,037 kg) and filled an area 10 feet (3 m) by 28 inches (71 cm). After the war, she would understand that she had been testing the B-29, the type of plane that would drop the atomic bomb.

In October 1944, Baumgartner made history again. The United States had been working on a new plane that would be powered by a jet-fueled engine. The plane was ready for testing, but the United States government wanted secrecy. When the YP-59A arrived at Wright Field, it had a false propeller so no one could tell that it was a jet. Once the jet was fired up for the test flight, the distinctive jet noise told the world what made the fighter fly.

Baumgartner's job during the test flight was to compare the speed, stability, and handling of the jet to that of other fighters. It turned out to have a stability problem that forced Baumgartner to correct the course. Adjustments would need to be made before the plane could be put into production. At the same time, she heard some disturbing news. The WASP program would be disbanded in December.

After the Disbanding of WASP

Between October, when the disbanding of WASP was announced, and December 1944, Baumgartner was given permission to fly in most of the planes she had not had a chance to try. She also tested a newly designed plane. Two P-51 plane fuselages were put together, separated by a wind section. The plane had two cockpits, one in each fuselage. The plane had been designed by an air force major named Bill Carl. The design turned out to be a success, as did the relationship between Baumgartner

Seven WASPs are shown here on an air field in Wilmington, Delaware, where they were sent to ferry planes. WASP members also helped train military pilots, towed targets for air force trainees, and acted as couriers.

and Carl. The two were married on May 12, 1945, five months after WASP disbanded.

They lived first in Virginia, then moved to Long Island, New York, in 1945, where Carl designed and built hydrofoil boats for the navy. He formed Dynamic Developments, Inc., a company that was eventually bought by Grumman Aerospace. He and Baumgartner had two children. After they were in school, Baumgartner went back to flying as an instructor and as a pilot for Dynamic Developments, Inc.

Baumgartner never got over her love of adventure. In 1977, after Carl retired from Grumman, he and Baumgartner sold all their possessions, even their house and cars, and bought a 45-foot

(14 m) sailing yacht. They spent the next two years sailing to Bermuda, Canada, Europe, throughout the Mediterranean, and the Caribbean. Baumgartner wrote a book about her adventures: *The Small World of Long-Distance Sailors.* Baumgartner passed away in March, 2008, just a month after her husband. She was eighty-nine years old.

Chronology

1939 **September 1** Adolf Hitler invades Poland.

September 3 In response to the invasion of Poland, Britain and France declare war on Nazi Germany, thus beginning World War II in Europe.

1941 **July** Jacqueline Cochran submits a plan for a women's air corps to General Hap Arnold.

December 7 Japan attacks the American naval base at Pearl Harbor, and the United States declares war.

December 11 Germany declares war on the United States.

1942 **March** Jackie Cochran and the twenty-five American women she recruited for the ATA travel to England.

May 15 The Women's Auxiliary Army Corps is established.

September Ten women, including Dorothy Swain, are chosen to take part in an experimental program for training women to be military flight instructors.

September 10 Secretary of War Henry L. Stimson announces the formation of the Women's Auxiliary Ferrying Squadron, with Nancy Harkness Love as director.

September 15 A training group for female pilots, the Women's Flying Training Detachment, is established, to be headed by Jackie Cochran.

October 19 The first pilots of the Women's Auxiliary Ferrying Squad begin ferrying aircraft and other munitions.

1943 July 1 The WAAC is converted to active military status and becomes the Women's Army Corps (WAC).

August 5 The WAFS and the WFTD merge to form the Women Airforce Service Pilots (WASP).

1944 February 19 A bill that would give WASP military status is introduced in Congress.

June 6 American, British, and Canadian troops land at Normandy, France, on what is today known as D-Day.

June 21 Congress defeats the bill to militarize WASP.

August 25 Paris is liberated by Allied forces.

October 3 WASP across the country receive letters announcing that they will be deactivated on December 20.

December 20 WASP is officially deactivated.

1945 February 13–15 The German city of Dresden is destroyed by firebombing.

April 16 Soviet troops begin their final assault on the German capital of Berlin.

April 30 Adolf Hitler commits suicide.

May 7 Germany surrenders to the Allied forces.

August 6 The atomic bomb is dropped on Hiroshima.

August 14 The Japanese agree to an unconditional surrender.

1953 Jacqueline Cochran becomes the first female pilot to fly faster than the speed of sound.

1977 President Jimmy Carter signs a bill honoring the members of the Women Airforce Service Pilots and granting them military status.

2005 The National WASP WWII Museum opens in Sweetwater, Texas.

2009 The WASP members are inducted into the International Air & Space Hall of Fame at the San Diego Air & Space Museum.

The WASP members are awarded the Congressional Gold Medal.

2015 The last surviving member of the first WASP training group, Betty Tackaberry Blake, passes away on April 9.

Chapter Notes

Chapter 4

Aircraft Tester Evelyn Sharp

1. Sarah Byrn Rickman, *The Originals: The Women's Auxiliary Ferrying Squadron of World War II*, (Sarasota, FL: Discus Books, 2001), p. 64.

Chapter 5

Dot Swain, the Artist Aviator

1. Winifred Wood and Dorothy Swain Lewis, *We Were WASPs* (Coral Gables, FL: Glade House, 1945).
2. Ann L. Cooper, *How High She Flies: Dorothy Swain Lewis* (Arlington Heights, IL: Aviatrix Publishing, 1999), p. 87.

Glossary

airmarking   Creating signs on the ground that can be seen from the air to aid in flight navigation.

aviator   Aircraft operator.

barnstormer   A pilot who performed acrobatics in the air, like wing-walking or parachute jumping. They were called barnstormers because they needed a farmer's field or pasture from which to stage their shows.

canopy   The glass or plastic cover of the pilot's compartment, including the windshield.

civilian   Nonmilitary, or when used as a noun, a nonmilitary person.

fuselage   The central body of an aircraft.

GI Bill   Passed in 1944, this bill provided financial assistance for education and training, loan guarantees for homes and farms, and job placement assistance to soldiers released from military service.

Great Depression   The worst economic collapse in the world, it lasted from 1929 until the early 1940s. Banks and businesses closed, leaving fifteen million Americans, nearly one-quarter of the workforce, without jobs.

jet airplane An aircraft powered by a jet engine, which, unlike a turboprop engine, uses the thrust generated by the combustion of fuel and oxygen to move forward.

Lend-Lease Act A bill passed in 1941 that allows the president to give aid to any country, as long as that country's defense is deemed important to the United States. After this act was passed during World War II, President Franklin Delano Roosevelt was able to give aid to Britain and the Soviet Union without the United States becoming directly involved in the war.

militarization Giving a person or group the status of being an official part of a country's military. Of great importance to the WASP, it would have given insurance benefits to the female pilots and made them veterans eligible for the provisions of the GI Bill.

munitions Weapons or other supplies necessary for carrying out warfare.

squadron A single unit of the military.

turboprop An engine that powers a propeller, where the propeller, not the engine itself, causes the movement of the aircraft.

war rationing During World War II, American citizens were allowed to purchase only a specific amount of items like food and gasoline. Supplying the troops was considered more important.

Women's Auxiliary Army Corps (WAAC)
Created in 1942, the WAAC filled noncombat jobs with women, freeing men for active service in combat. Initially, the women were hired as civilian employees. In 1943, the word "Auxiliary" was dropped, and the WAC became part of the military.

zoot suit A suit intentionally cut to be very baggy and large, with shoulder pads and narrow pantcuffs.

Bibliography

Bartels, Diane Ruth Armour. *Sharpie: The Life Story of Evelyn Sharp.* Lincoln, NE: Dageforde Publishing, 1996.

Carl, Ann B. *A WASP Among Eagles: A Military Test Pilot in World War II.* Washington, DC: Smithsonian Institution, 1999.

Cochran, Jacqueline. *The Stars at Noon.* Boston: Little Brown, 1954.

Cochran, Jacqueline. *Jackie Cochran: The Autobiography of the Greatest Woman Pilot in Aviation History.* New York, NY: Bantam, 1987.

Cole, Jean Hascall. *Women Pilots of World War II.* Salt Lake City, UT: University of Utah Press, 2002.

Cooper, Ann L. *How High She Flies: Dorothy Swain Lewis.* Arlington Heights, IL: Aviatrix Publishing, 1999.

Keil, Sally Van Wagenen. *Those Wonderful Women in Their Flying Machines: The Unknown Heroines of World War II.* New York, NY: Four Directions Press, 1979.

Nathan, Amy. *Yankee Doodle Gals: Women Pilots of World War II.* Washington, DC: National Geographic, 2001.

Nolen, Stephanie. *Promised the Moon: The Untold Story of the First Women in the Space Race.* New York, NY: Four Walls Eight Windows, 2002.

O'Brien, Keith. *Fly Girls: How Five Daring Women Defied All Odds and Made Aviation History.* New York, NY: Eamon Dolan/Houghton Mifflin Harcourt, 2018.

Rickman. Sarah Byrn. *The Originals: Women's Auxiliary Ferrying Squadron of World War II.* Sarasota, FL: Discus Books, 2001.

Rickman, Sarah Byrne. *WASP of the Ferry Command: Women Pilots, Uncommon Deeds.* Denton, TX: University of North Texas Press, 2016.

Further Reading

Books

Barlow, Col. Cassie, and Sue Norrod. *Saluting Our Grandmas: Women of World War II*. Gretna, LA: Pelican Publishing, 2017.

Garstecki, Julia. *WASPs (All-American Fighting Forces)*. Mankato, MN: Black Rabbit Books, 2016.

O'Brien, Keith. *Fly Girls: How Five Daring Women Defied All Odds and Made Aviation History*. New York, NY: Eamon Dolan/Houghton Mifflin Harcourt, 2018.

Pearson, P. O'Connell. *Fly Girls: The Daring American Women Pilots Who Helped Win WWII*. Reprint edition. New York, NY: Simon & Schuster Books for Young Readers, 2019.

Simons, Lisa M. Bolt. *The U.S. WASP: Trailblazing Women Pilots of World War II*. Mankato, MC: Capstone Press, 2017.

Ure, James. *Seized by the Sun: The Life and Disappearance of World War II Pilot Gertrude Tompkins*. Chicago, IL: Chicago Review Press, 2017.

Websites
The Bullock Texas State History Museum
www.thestoryoftexas.com
The Bullock Museum, located in Austin, Texas, has lots of information and educational resources on its website, including archived stories in the Texas Story Project, images of artifacts, and articles on WASP and their base in Sweetwater.

National Women's History Museum
www.womenshistory.org
The website for the National Women's History Museum in Alexandria, Virginia, offers digitized exhibits, articles, and other resources about women throughout American history.

National World War II Museum
www.nationalww2museum.org
The National World War II Museum is a museum located in New Orleans, Louisiana, dedicated to showcasing the history of the United States' involvement in World War II, and its website includes student resources, profiles on key figures, and the ability to search its collections.

Index